THE BEAUTIFUL ONES

BEAUTY FOR ASHES

THE BEAUTIFUL ONES

Amie Clemonds	Pamela King	Nikki Randolph
Lisa Tompkins	Pauletta Fields	Tameya Banks
Ann Bush-Curry	Cynthia Roberts	Stacey L. Fields

Table of Contents

Lady Winnetta Whittier

FOREWORD

Remembering testimony service, we used to go to church every Friday and Sunday night. That was the highlight of a Christian's walk with the Lord. People couldn't wait to tell what the Lord had done! Testimonies of victory through Jesus Christ caused the glory of the Lord to fill the sanctuary and the saints would break out with praise! Our testimonies of faith helped us to build our hope in Jesus Christ our Lord. When we hear of the victories of our fellow laborers, it encourages us to keep our faith and trust in Him. Evangelist Stacey Lynn Fields brings that atmosphere back to life in this book of triumph called "The Beautiful Ones!" These are women who have risen above the ashes of their past, becoming the Queens they were created to be! The one thing they all have in common, which is necessary to possess and to produce victory in your lives is having a trusting relationship with God, our Heavenly Father. As the Word of God says, "They overcame him (the adversary) by the blood of the Lamb, and by the word of their testimony." **(Revelation 12:11)**

We all have a story to tell and we all have shared some of the same outcomes of victory. That is why you will be able to relate to the testimonies in this book. You too will rejoice after hearing of the divine restorations that these writers have experienced in their lives! No matter how sinful you were or how far away from God you felt you were, God's love was able to reach way down to a level that was too low to be reached by man. Through life's ups and downs, from depression to disappointment and from temptations to trials, we who put our trust in God will have testimonies of victory through Jesus Christ! **(1 Corinthians 15:57)** But thanks be to God, which giveth us the victory through our Lord Jesus Christ.

The Beautiful Ones

Evangelist Stacey L. Fields is a woman who is persistent when it comes to accomplishing any task set before her. She is a woman of her word and is very dependable especially when it comes to serving in the Lord's House. She is a woman whose greatest work is—Helps! **(1 Corinthians 12:28)** She possesses many gifts and is capable of doing what she set out to do no matter how difficult it may seem to others. She is very optimistic and is supported by her tremendous faith in our God! Bringing to you these testimonies of faith will inspire you to think of the Goodness of the Lord and testify of the victories He has won—then you will find that you are one of the:
"The Beautiful Ones!"

Amie

Philippians 4:13
I can do ALL things through Christ who strengthens me.

Love Out Loud

I believe that everything that has happened to me in life is what led me to believing and having a trusting relationship with God. I didn't grow up in the best household. My mother did what she could, but I had an abusive father, who is bi-polar, which prompted me to move out when I was 18. My mother taught me to always be independent and never let anyone take care of you, so I took that to heart, I moved out. Over time I got married, we had three beautiful boys, one which is in Heaven.

It was the year 2005 that set the tone for the following years. I lost my baby, James, in July of 2005. Three months later, my brother was injured in Iraq. It felt like after that, all we ever received was bad news. My dad had a multiple strokes, but by then my mom and dad had gotten divorced. My mom had moved to a different state and been there for years. I did have two boys and a husband that loved me, but I always felt that I was missing a piece of my heart.

I spiraled into depression as a result of severe bi-polar, gained 50lbs, and finally one day I walked out of a terrible job where I was working. I stayed at home for a few months, but what's the saying? When one door closes, another one opens. I landed a new job and had no idea what road this would lead me to.

On my first day I met a lady named Stacey. Now, I'm blonde and loud with lots of tattoos and cussed like a sailor. She was the complete opposite of me. A few years older ☺, she was very quiet, polite, didn't cuss and had no tattoos. But, I knew from the beginning

3

our souls matched.

We took a road trip to a conference and had the best time getting to know each other. After that the rest was history. She became my soul sister. Eventually, she moved onto a better job and so did I but we always kept in contact. I had been at my job for a little over a year, I was feeling better mentally and physically. I lost weight. I bought a new house. But, still felt like something was missing.

One day out of the blue, Stacey calls me. She tells me that she woke up with a message from God she needed to tell me. Now, I can't remember each and everything she said to me that day, but I do remember asking her, "Who have you talked to?" It was literally like someone was reading my mind. She talked about all the thoughts I was having, even though I hadn't told anyone. It was like she knew it all. She told me that God wanted me to go to Church and that we (me and God) needed to have a better relationship.

When I got off the phone I was crying. How can she know everything that is going on in my head? So that night, I decided to find a church. I went that Sunday and the feeling I had when I walked in was overwhelming. I was emotional; It was like getting a hug from a loved one. I felt my grandma for the first time in years. She was telling me I was home. When the minister spoke, it's like he is speaking straight to my heart; still to this day.

I didn't always have the best life. I was mentally losing myself, having thoughts that no one should have, fighting demons within myself. I was making wrong decisions. It was like I was drowning and get couldn't out of the water. I had put myself in such a depression I couldn't get out of. I was looking everywhere to find what happiness is, but never thought to look above the clouds.

HE was looking for me, HE was reaching out to me. I couldn't hear him because I was so down and lost that he went to my sister for help. I'm so blessed that HE did this for me. I feel like I'm a new person now. With God at my back, I can do anything. When I am feeling sad, depressed or just thankful, I know I can reach out to him and He will ALWAYS guide me. He is there when I need him. For so long, all I could look at was the negative. But with Jesus, He shows me the sunlight in every day. He shows me the blessings I have and when I get to Heaven He will introduce me to my Son. I thank God every day for reaching out to me.

Pamela

James 1:12 (NIV)
Blessed is the one who perseveres under trial because, having stood the test, that person will receive the crown of life that the Lord has promised to those who love him.

Confessions from a Mended Crown: The Lies, Facts, and Truths about Healing

Hello Gorgeous! I am honored to share my story of healing with you, while living my blessed life, knowing the best is yet to come! I am called to serve God's people as a minister of reconciliation for those whose mind, body, and spirit has been broken by the hardships of life. I speak life into their brokenness as they seek healing from the inside out and experience God's divine restoration. I use those same gifts in business, as a leadership coach and consultant to empower courageous women to embrace bold steps to success without guilt, shame, or fear!

Before I fully embraced the call on my life, I served over 20 years in the United States Air Force, founded a nonprofit to support survivors of domestic violence and sexual assault survivors, and then served as the Strategic Engagement Leader of a four-state region for a national nonprofit that teaches people how to listen with empathy.

But, before I could speak life into the broken and discouraged people God sent my way, I first had to face my own feelings of guilt, shame, and fear. Those feelings started in 1989, when I was eleven years old, and a stranger broke into my house and raped me. Back then, counseling was reserved for the people in my neighborhood who were labeled as "crazy. " Children didn't talk about those kinds of things, especially outside of the home. I was told not to worry, eventually I would forget it happened and the nightmares would go away on their own – just give it some time. And so, I let time heal my ravaged body, confused mind, broken heart, lack of trust, fear of darkness, and dreams of becoming of princess that were destroyed that night. I became so independent that I learned not to rely on anyone to keep my safe. I also refused to be anyone's victim again, especially men.

Not long after I was raped, while walking the hallways of middle school, a little boy came up behind me and popped my bra strap. Before I could react, he smacked me on the butt as he walked past me in the hallway at school. The next thing I remember, I was standing over him as he laid on the floor crying and holding his crotch. Moments later, I was sitting in the principal's office being disciplined for assaulting him as my gym teacher and mother defended me and kept the school administrators from suspending me. I was instructed by the principal to apologize to him and his mother for hurting him. I chose my words very carefully and apologized for exactly what I felt sorry for – not being his victim and that I had to be the one to teach him how to treat little girls. I learned a lot that day about safety, security, and fairness. Life would teach me about trust and justice, I just had to keep being strong and wait for time to hopefully heal me.

Fast forward through time, through moments in my life, when I was scared to be alone at night and could barely sleep through the night without a light on. Can I tell you about the moments when I almost elbowed a customer service rep who walked up behind me to ask me if I needed help? Or maybe the nightmares of what I would do to anyone who hurt me? Oh, I can't forget to tell you about my independent woman phase of purchasing a car without asking anyone for guidance and paid three times its value but couldn't get rid of it after the engine died less than a year after I bought it. And still I refused to ask for help, because I could take care of myself, and I did not need anyone to fix my problems. People said I was strong and brave, but the truth was, I was broken at my core.

And then it happened, the summer of 2008 when all the trauma I experienced in my life, the trauma that time was supposed to heal, finally hit me. I was lost, in every sense of the word. I was less than a mile from my house, but somehow, I had zoned out and had no idea where I was, how long I was gone, what direction I was headed, and nothing around me looked familiar. I was terrified; my heart racing, my head spinning, my cell phone dead, and I was spiraling out of control. Time had betrayed me. I needed real healing, from the inside out. This kind of healing took more than strength. It took faith to believe I could be healed. It took prayer to not give up. It took courage to ask for help and yes, it took time to walk through months of trauma therapy. Through this walk of faith, spiritual support, and professional help, I learned how to own my story and replace guilt, shame, and fear with truth, authenticity, and resilience.

In 2009, I was sharing my journey of healing to encourage other victims to seek help, using all that I learned to encourage and inspire them in their own journeys. By 2012, I was telling my story and advocating for others to seek healing, hope, and justice they needed to feel whole. It was then I realized, I was no longer angry about what happened to me because my peace of mind was not based on finding the person who raped me or getting justice through a courtroom. I realized that no matter what was taken from me, what I longed for was victory over victimization. But that is not where this story ends. In 2018, God said I was ready. Twenty-nine years to-the-date, I met the man who committed the crime against me in 1989. I was a gladiator in the courtroom, standing in the arena of justice, when he was sentenced to thirty-five years in prison. I walked in that courtroom as more than a conqueror, because God healed me from the inside out and allowed me to face my past and speak confidently about the woman I became, despite the hurt and brokenness he created. In that moment, I knew I was whole.

The Beautiful Ones

This was not the life (nor challenges) I imagined for myself when I was growing up, but I would not change a thing. You see, all these battles turned into victories, because I did not have to fight them alone. They have shaped me into the bold, courageous, fiery, feisty, brave, and fearless woman I am today, just as God created me to be. It took some time, but I finally realized, I am hard-wired to stand as a victorious witness for God's toughest battles. But that does not mean I do not get tired of fighting, that my scars do not hurt, that I do not cry in surrender to God on my difficult days and moments of fatigue. It just means that I refuse to give up, I will not give in, I will not back down. I have figured out the secret to winning every battle, war, and challenge I face – I just have to show up! I already know the outcome – I am going to win! But I must step into the ring, to raise my arms in victory, so that weary eyes, broken hearts, hopeless minds, and lost souls, can see for themselves what is possible with God. They will see me get knocked down but not get knocked out. They will see me bruised and scarred, but not shattered nor destroyed. And every time I get back up, God gets the glory!

So as God restored the mind I thought I was losing, he also released me from the anger that consumed me. God replaced my fears of darkness with peace so that I could rest and sleep at night. He unclenched the fist I would instinctively make when men came too close and startled me. He also mended the broken mindset of the extremely independent woman I believed I had to have to be successful. As much as I love being right, I am so glad I was wrong about that!

Confession time! If you want to be healed, if you want to be restored, if you want to walk in victory, you must separate facts from truths from lies. You see, facts are the results of what we can prove. Truths are the evidence of what we believe. Lies are the stories we tell ourselves when we deny the facts and ignore our truths. It is important to catch that, so read those statements again and let that sink in before I slice up and serve you this next big revelation (insert sarcasm). There are some lies that come masked as facts that will have our truths all twisted up, leaving us consumed with guilt, shame, and fear. Pretty soon, we will start to believe we are not worthy, the egregious acts of violence that happened to us in either childhood or adulthood are our faults, that we are not worthy of love, that we are not capable of achieving our goals, that we must settle for less, and that we do not deserve the fullness of life that we envisioned as little girls – lies, lies, lies!

Now let me share with you the truths I've learned in my healing journey, found in the book of **Romans, Chapter 8**:
1. Bad things do happen to good people (**Roman 8:1-17**)
2. Brokenness comes in all shapes, sizes, ages, and phases in life (**Romans 8:18-27**)
3. Invisible scars are real, and time will not heal them (**Romans 8:28-30**)
4. Even though your wounds are healed, sometimes the scars remain (**Romans 8:31-39**)

Today, I have been married to the man of my dreams for nearly 20 years and our amazing children are thriving despite COVID-19 as they pursue their hopes and dreams. Do not get me wrong, in my heart, I am still a little girl from a single-wide trailer on bricks, nestled in a trailer park with no paved roads, crushed seashells, a few stop signs, and no stop lights, who loved chewing on sugar canes, with cuts on my little legs from the raspberry patches. I was born bossy, with my hands on my hips, an answer for everything, and ready to take on the whole wide world! I have learned so much as I grew from a self-declared princess into the daughter of the Most High King (God) and who also happened to marry a King (my hubby). The crown I wear is full of pearls of wisdom, diamonds from the rough battles, and rubies for the blood of Christ that runs through my veins that has made me whole. My crown is not light, but my burdens are no longer heavy. It may not be shiny, but its polished. It is not for riches, but for God's Glory. It was once broken, but it is now healed. And if you ever see it crooked, please do not hesitate to tell me in truth and in love – Queen, you need to adjust your crown!

Nikki

2 Timothy 2:15

Do your best to present yourself to God as one approved, a worker who does not need to be ashamed and who correctly handles the word of truth.

Girls like You

It rained the day I met her. Tashina Phillips stepped right out of the passenger's side of her husband's car and right into my life as my new best friend, well at least for a short chapter of my life.

It was the first day of Biology class at the Junior College. I was attending to obtaining my Bachelor's degree in Organizational Studies. I originally flunked the course the semester prior and not passing this time around was just not an option. I planned to rush through the course and back to my studies at Saint Louis University. Just the thought of passing the course at half the price made me the happiest girl on earth.

We all stood outside of the class buying time until the professor graced us with his or her presence. When a gray Chrysler 300 pulled up quickly, a woman seem to have gotten out just as quickly, fumbling her books and umbrella before the driver skirted off. I had no choice but to look over towards the woman who was a lot similar to me but seemed to be crying. I tried to make eye contact with her.

"Are you okay?" I asked covering her with my umbrella, as she struggled to open her umbrella while wiped away her tears.

"Oh I'm fine, my husband is just stupid," she said pretending her tears were just raindrops that so happen to have fallen from the sky onto her face.

I was skeptical of talking to her any further; I mean, she could have easily told me that she didn't want to be bothered. Some find my company a tad bit overwhelming considering I am always so social. I find it very hard to pretend to be an introvert. As a social butterfly, smiling and making small-talk came as second nature to me. I called it my gift of gab, just a little one of God's blessings He bestowed unto me. Tashina on the other hand seemed to have needed a little motivation in that department. Even after I had held my umbrella over her while she juggled her books, jacket, tears, and umbrella, she still seemed to not make eye contact with me. I wasn't surprised though. After disclosing something so personal, what did I expect, for her to break into a big song and dance about her marriage with a complete stranger? Plus, would I even want to know all of that? How crazy would this woman be to have continued to tell me how her husband made her cry?

So there we were, sitting two seats apart from each other in the stadium-style lecture hall once a week, working to make passing grades for a professor who only known us as mere numbers on an attendance roster. Days progressed and Tashina and I grew closer and closer as friends. Our seats grew closer and closer in distance. The exchange of candy bars and potato chips was considered as a token of friendship with each class passing into a semester of celebrity gossip and getting to know each other. Tashina liked crunchy snickers, while I found munching on peanut M&Ms made the class go by faster.

By the end of the semester, I had spent most of my evenings talking to Tashina on the phone catching each other up on television shows we shared a liking for, talking about friends, churches, experiences, and relationships. The subject of Tashina's tumultuous marriage and how her husband mistreated her after he received a better job came up quite often. It was funny how we would talk about a funny episode of Friends which resulted in how lucky Rachel was that Ross wasn't needy like her husband Greg during their time of dating, or how Martin and Gina's relationship was nothing like the relationship she had with Greg and how she wished he was as funny as Martin when things went wrong.

The unhappy couple first met when Tashina began working two jobs to pay off the debt from a past boyfriend that abused her credit and cheated on her. After breaking up with this loser, she met Greg, a security guard at a shipyard. Greg was once mesmerized by Tashina's maturity as a hard-working payroll clerk by day and creative jewelry salesman by night. However, the spark seemed to have dimed right after the two got married and Tashina's father, a retired Detective, helped Greg into the police academy.

With Greg working in the public so much, he seemed to receive more attention than he bargained for. He had more confidence than when working the shipyard. With all the heroic admiration and extra attention Greg received from the ladies, Tashina grew accustomed to nights alone. Her husband would purposely pick fights, constantly putting her down, because she didn't dress like any of the girls he watched while patrolling the night clubs; all the while with an overnight bag tucked conveniently under the bed.

I felt sad for Tashina. I tried comforting her with my own life as a single mother whose recent engagement to the father of my child was called off due to my unwillingness to settle for less. Being an ambitious twenty-five-year-old, I had purchased my first home on my own and looked forward to racing closer towards my career in Human Resources after college. Tashina motivated me and constantly made me feel as if I was the only one she could call a friend, except for the times I would talk to her about my dating life.

"It was so much fun Tashina, we went to the movies and out to dinner, but I don't see any longevity in this," I said, tucking myself under my covers after a long night on the town, dreading Tashina's response.

"Well, girls like you need to just be cautious with dating. You know when I was dating Greg I was just getting over a bad relationship I had just came out of and so," Tashina would say. Her reoccurring stories seem to always trail from her glory days of dating Greg before he turned into a complete nightmare of a husband, while forgetting the phrase "girls like you", was completely off-putting considering I was only four years younger than her. Although the phrase would make my eyes roll and the thought of her giving me advice about relationships made me sick to my stomach. I mean, I enjoyed talking to Tashina, but she and I didn't attract the same guys, so how could she advise me of anything? I was a different type of girl alright; girls like me didn't let men abuse them whatsoever. I would have dropped Greg down to size a long time ago.

It gave me pleasure to know that I had someone who had dated just as much as I did in the past and could give some sound advice seeing my mistakes outside myself. I only wished my vast courtships and constant dates would have promoted a better outlook on her starting over. The grass IS greener on the other side, shoot, there's grass period versus the stone she'd seem to have been sleeping next to at night. I mean, come on, I know that in every relationship there is more than one side to a story, but her husband was downright cruel. Some of the responses that were said to her in passing while I was on the phone were borderline abusive. Like the time Greg watched porn in front of Tashina and told her that she should take notes or the first time I met him Greg completely disregarded my handshake and mocked the way Tashina was dressed instead. While my hand was still extended he called her names and said that she looked a mess. How was this woman putting up with this, and why? Most importantly why wouldn't she tell her father or her three younger brothers to step in for help?

Tashina was old school; I guess the thought of someone from her family being involved in her marriage was embarrassing and degrading. Tashina must've wanted to be the one to make things right in her marriage. I could tell by the way she spoke about other women in her family, making mention they were all single and their statistics. I guessed divorce wasn't an option. Tashina felt being married made her something special and being single or divorced would have made her a sad case or unwanted just like they were. Or like I was to her, I guess.

"The women in my family don't even believe in marriage Nikki," she would say, "girls like you should really try to find the right man because these men out here aren't trying to do right or get married, they just want to play around. It's slim picking out there," she would repeat. I always wanted to respond with a quick, "How would you know? You're too busy getting verbally abused to know what's out here in the dating world. When was the last time you went on a date? When was the last time you actually kissed Greg? Or rather, when was the last time he actually kissed you? Was it when he still desperately needed someone to rescue him from the shipyard or was it the day I met you and he made you cry in class? Pretty sure you wish your father never introduced him to a real job huh?"

The thought of speaking to her that way satisfied my mind for only a split second, before I returned backed to my right mind and reminded myself I was her friend and friends don't speak that way. The thought alone made me sick to my stomach, not because it made me a bad friend, but in that headspace I was as abusive as her husband. That nasty thought alone would inevitably create a response that would finally seep out of my mouth one day adding the worst taste to our friendship. The Bible says to be quick to listen, slow to speak, and slow to become angry. My quick wit and fast temper would do nothing, but create a wedge between us.

I was twenty when I had my son and since then, I had found myself nothing more than a mean bully at times or what I called, "A Mama Bear." Work colleagues feared me and anyone outside of my circle annoyed me. I was mean for sport at times and didn't know why. As for family, I wanted to raise my son the way I wanted to with no help at all from other influences including my son's grandparents. My son was very fortunate to have all four grandparents to lean on, but it was made very clear that he was my son and I would raise him as I saw fit. Any questions and off with your head, I was the only queen of my castle and visitation hours in my son's life were limited, if you were not aware of my wrath.

Then it happened, I was at work one afternoon when Tashina called me like she normally does when she didn't want to go home from work. She sounded so exhausted but, scared.

"Nikki, how are you?" Tashina said, with a sudden shrill to her voice.

"Tashina, what's wrong?" I asked as I turned my chair towards the phone to give her my undivided attention. I wanted to be there with her, even if it was just to hug her and tell her everything would be okay. I probably would've left my job if she started to cry, I was only two weeks away from my last day in my position anyway. I was transferring to another hospital and happily awaiting my last day.

"Nikki I know we haven't known each other for very long, but I wanted to see if you would be interested in going on a spiritual trip with me in Atlanta," Tashina sat silently awaiting my response, preparing herself for my decline.

Every time I began to speak she would start speaking again to throw some new bargaining tool or information in that would hopefully gain my approval to go. Little did she know that I was hoping for a way to use up the rest of the little vacation time I had left.

"It's called MegaFest, it's sponsored by TD Jakes and The Potter House. We can drive down there, we can go in my SUV, I will do all the driving," she muttered.

"Tashina, of course, I will go with you. I love to travel," I said marking my calendar. Our trip would discontinue the day of my new employee physical for my new job. The return would be rushed, but I didn't care. I was so pleased with Tashina's invitation. Tashina could have asked anyone on earth to go with her but, I was her choice. The date we were planning to leave would be her birthday. I closed my eyes and clutched my pearls in awe of being the friend she could depend on. That week, I packed feeling no longer as a classmate, but a best friend.

*   *   *

The day of the trip came as quickly as the week ended and I was all smiles when Tashina picked me up for our trip to Atlanta. I rushed to the car with my short blue halter dress on, my overnight bag, and a birthday gift for Tashina. I bought Tashina a journal in hopes that I would be giving her the answer to her prayers, a way to jot down her thoughts and fears. Journaling always made me decipher my thoughts in the past. With all the relationships and broken promises I had been through, my journals had always been there for me to write down my deepest darkest thoughts.

At this point, some of the things Tashina said of her marriage only belonged in a journal and the ride to Atlanta only made it worst. As Tashina drove vigorously down the highways and byways she spoke of Greg's numerous infidelities and how he constantly compared her to the girls in the club. I listened intently trying to match her stories with my own experiences, but I had never actually been in a bad relationship for very long. My selfishness and self-loathing had only granted me enough patience to leave a relationship as soon as I wasn't happy. I guess, that's why girls like me weren't married, I thought. Satan and his self-doubt seemed to have triggered me often lately. I couldn't wait to get to MegaFest.

"We need to stop and get gas," Tashina said as we veered off the highway exit. I went over to the gas station attendant and paid for our gas. On the way back Tashina seemed perplexed. She eyed me up and down with a puzzling look.

"Nikki, you okay?" she asked as I pumped the gas. I nodded and smiled as Tashina turned off the engine and got out of the car with the same baffled look on her face.

"Nikki, are you feeling okay?" she asked looking me up and down.

"Yes, of course, do I look okay?" I asked as Tashina pulled on my halter dress.

"Yes you look fine, but that dress doesn't look the same as it did a couple of hours ago," Tashina said as she continued to size me up,

"It's hot today, I been sweating a lot," I said wiping the sweat from my brow. It was a hot day. It was the first week of July and boy was I anxious to get to Atlanta to lay down a bit and so was Tashina. Tashina made mention she felt nauseous. The sun beating down on us both made our trip to Atlanta almost unbearable, but we had gotten there with hopes we would feel better the next day.

The next day Tashina had a complete day of gospel conferences for us to attend. It was beautiful. T. D. Jakes and a long list of gospel guests and comedians filled the arena with joy and happiness. You could feel the passion in the air of hopeful Christians praying for a chance to change and shape their lives in some way to get closer to God. I had been to a bunch of concerts but nothing like this. Christ's message was spread amongst the masses, anointing each of us with the Holy Spirit. People of all ages, races, colors, and creeds crying, laughing, and enjoying God's Word together. Wow, what a beautiful sight to see. The arena felt like what Heaven would be, nothing but happiness and singing, laughter, most of all love for one another. My small church back home of twenty-five members felt like a small family picnic compared to MegaFest. It was amazing.

Tashina and I stayed in the nicest hotel on Peachtree just ten minutes away from the conferences. That weekend I taught Tashina how to swim and we even got a chance to take a tour of Martin

Luther King's burial, museum, his church, as well as his early residence.

Our days were filled with such fun and laughter while our nights were filled with complete confusion. Tashina and I were battling something we both couldn't explain. Each night I would wake up to a puddle of sweat. On my way to the restroom, I would slide out of bed and ring my nightgown out into a pool of water. Too tired, confused, and embarrassed to ask if I peed in my bed or was running a fever. It was neither. I would change my nightgown and would go back to sleep to find Tashina waking up an hour later each night to throw up. Tashina would blame her upchuck on what we had for dinner the night before. But, back at MegaFest we would go each day for our daily conferences and concerts. We would feel wonderful until we had to report back to our room for the evening for bed. We thought it was the room so we switch rooms twice but the curse seemed to still follow. The entire time that we spent in Atlanta we were fine outside of the room but each night brought us closer and closer to unexplained illnesses. By adjusting the air conditioning, our diets, and pajamas, Tashina and I spent each night trying to remedy what we thought was a cursed room.

The last and final day of the conference brought me to tears. It was as if T. D. Jakes was speaking directly to me. For the remainder of the trip, I felt a ray of light awaken my soul like no other. Other than the night sweats and Tashina throwing up each night, I had a remarkable time. When we returned home from our trip I felt my internal self awaken and shed the negative spirit within me. I no longer wanted to be that bullying mean spirited woman that made excuses for or that unfair and unloving girl that I aspired to be at work. I had made up my mind that I would leave my current job and transfer with the understanding that I would be an exemplary performer in my next position and would love and care for my job until I was in my career no matter what. My son's grandparents would know what days would be best to visit him and I would set loving and flexible boundaries for us all. I was a changed woman, in more ways than one.

When Tashina and I returned to St. Louis, nothing was ever the same. That same week I went to Cardinal Glennon Hospital to sign my acceptance letter and complete my employee physical. My TB test came back as positive that week and I couldn't start the job without a chest x-ray and a visit from my doctor who was responsible for giving me the bad news that I had cancer, Non-Hodgkins Lymphoma to be exact.

That same week Tashina came home from the trip to find Greg more loving and understanding than ever. After making love to her husband twice that morning, he decided to reach over in his nightstand to hand Tashina divorce papers. "You had two times to please me and you couldn't even do that. I want a divorce," Greg said as he handed Tashina a pen. The date on the divorce decree shown Greg had filed on Tashina's birthday which was the day we were at MegaFest.

Broken-hearted we both called each other in tears wondering what the future would hold. I was only twenty-five years old with a five-year-old son who would grow up without a mother. I had a brand new car, a mortgage and couldn't fully start work because I had chemo and doctor's visits to attend. Tashina had packed her bags awaiting the best time to tell her mother, aunts, and grandmother about Greg's requests for a divorce until she took a pregnancy test and decided to stay married to Greg.

Things were never the same. The class ended and I barely passed. Tashina and I didn't speak as much. Sharing bad to worst news back and forth was daunting and the feeling of judgment for staying with someone who asked for a divorce made it hard for Tashina to speak to me after I called her husband everything but a child of God, thinking the coast was clear since he was divorcing her.

Creating another outlet for us both, I introduced Tashina to my other friends. Pregnant Tashina wasn't as happy as, "free to leave whenever she wanted Tashina." I, on the other hand, after losing over thirty pounds got closer to God and decided to take obituary pictures. I turned twenty-six years old weighing only a hundred and nine pounds while my six-year-old son went to therapy after kindergarten classes to learn how to deal with my sickness. At this point I did not mind knowing that I was dying, I just didn't want to look like I was. The horror in my father's and son's eyes made it impossible to give up. I received Chemo through a port in my chest and asked my father to shave my head. My mother knew I was strong and that I would be okay. My father broke down occasionally and refused to shave my head. Luckily, I didn't lose much hair and radiation went well.

Later that summer I met my husband and Tashina was the first of my friends I told. I was so excited to tell her since I felt she was on the journey with me the entire time. We had gotten engaged over dinner before going Christmas shopping. The whole restaurant knew he was about to pop the question and they all stood up and applauded when I sobbed out, "Yes."

Things were starting to get back to normal in my life, however Tashina was nowhere around. I was now cancer free and getting married. Yeah, Tashina may have helped me with my wedding and was a good sounding board during my Bridezilla moments, but she just wasn't there like I felt she was before. I know she was pregnant and had her own life to live but I was so happy. I wanted her to be happy with me. She was my Maid of Honor and ended up my wedding planner when all failed. I knew Tashina was unhappy at home, but I made sure to not judge or really ask about it. There wasn't anything I could do at this time to fix any of the situations she chose to be in, nor could I take back the words I once said about Greg when he presented divorce documents to her in bed. I hated Greg, I prayed every night to deliver me from that hate and forgive me for my sins. God presented his answer more than once.

Tashina and Greg had a pregnancy photo shoot, then a baby

shower. I came to the shower feeling like a horrible friend. Yes, I had bought a gift, but Tashina had a long list of friends that planned and executed her big day. She and Greg moved out of their apartment and into their first home, Tashina didn't accept my proposal to help them pack. During my wedding Tashina mentioned she didn't know what she was doing being my Maid of Honor. I guess she didn't think we had been friends long enough for her to be in that position. I sat at my wedding in shock at her speech, considering I didn't think there could ever be a better person for that position. I could only have two bridesmaids and I guess I was wrong in thinking that the trip to Atlanta meant more than a mere road trip. The trip to Atlanta was God-lead, to me. I felt God placed me in Tashina's path to bring me closer to HIM. I seemed to have made the mistake of thanking Tashina for the trip to Atlanta instead of thanking God. I continued to try to make plans with Tashina once I returned from my honeymoon, but scheduling time with a new mother was almost impossible. Then the other shoe fell.

A group of my friends went out to dinner for my friend Ann's birthday. We were seated right up front in the first booth of the restaurant. Later a couple sat in the booth behind us. After over an hour of gossiping, laughing, and catching up, I stood up to find the restroom. The booth was so close to ours, when I stood up I noticed I could have bumped heads with the gentleman sitting right behind me. After two double takes, I noticed the man was Greg. Tashina's husband was with another woman, half-dressed, younger woman to be exact.

"Oh wow, hi Greg," I exclaimed leaning over their table, "where my friend at?"

"At home," Greg said as he rolled his eyes matter-of-factly. I looked over at the young lady adjusting her halter top and her micro mini shorts looking not phased at all. I went to the restroom and called Tashina right away. I could hear the baby in the background crying as she began to say hello.

"Tashina, it's Nikki. I'm here at dinner with my friends and guess who's sitting in the booth right behind me?" Tashina sat silent. I almost didn't want to say.

"Oh, that's a shame," Tashina muttered as I followed back up with support.

"Girl me and my friends are here, you want us to jump him?" I quizzed as Tashina continued to say it was a shame.

She rushed off the phone to tend to the baby. I left the bathroom and later the restaurant with my friends knowing I really needed to close this chapter of my life. Tashina was completely finished with our friendship; she had bigger fish to fry. I prayed nightly for Tashina and her family, hoping God would bind the enemy and deliver her from any hurt, harm or danger. Leaving that friendship in good standing as a personal blessing to gain a real relationship with God as I desperately needed to back then. No more negative thoughts or mean spirits surrounded me. I was a happy, spiritually healthy young woman that had reconciled my relationship with God through the trip with Tashina.

About a year and half later I saw Tashina in the mall. I was with some friends from church and decided to go into the bookstore where I saw her pick up a magazine and start heading to the cash register. Her daughter was old enough to sit up firmly in a stroller. I rushed over to greet her and her daughter and felt the coldness of her glare. I gave them both a hug before even looking down at what Tashina was purchasing. In Tashina's hand held a King Magazine, I would assume for her husband. Tashina looked embarrassed and then decided not to look at me at all. We said our goodbyes and I never spoke to her ever again. I was able to walk away from Tashina with my head held high knowing God brought us together for a purpose. I fulfilled my purpose as her great friend who taught her to swim, that shoulder to cry on and ear when she trusted no one with her marriage problems, not even her mother. Tashina introduced me to my truth. I needed to change my mind, my thoughts and most importantly my behavior, but unfortunately it took going on a spiritual journey and cancer to do so, but I am not ashamed. Tashina holding the magazine for her husband, should not be ashamed either. Tashina should sit in her truth and know God has a plan. I hope wherever Tashina is today, she knows God has a plan, she's sees the truth of that plan, and she has been delivered for that plan.

Lisa

2 Timothy 2:15
Greater is He that is in me than he that is in the world.

Self Esteem

For so many years I battled with having low self esteem. It took me until I was 41yrs old to realize this and step into a new life and new understanding of myself and most of all love me. I grew up in an era where the girls with the good shape or big booty got the attractive guys. I was tall straight up and down with no kinda shape. So anytime I was shown attention from a boy I looked at it as hey they see me. They think I'm cute. So I would let them feel my but, when I walked pass them. I never looked at it as a violation, I thought it was something good cause I was finally seen by a boy. And not just any boy the popular boy.

My mom worked a lot so, I mostly was home alone with my lil sister. After school I walked to the daycare center to pick her up. Well, one day on my way there I met Rob. Rob was what every young girl in that era liked; he was light skin, had a long jerry curl, and a 9/8 car. Around the corner from Rob was this boy name Tyrone. Tyrone hard smooth dark skin a nice body, low cut waves, and a sexy smile with a solid gold tooth in the front. For me to get his attention I thought I really hit the jackpot. What I didn't know was Rob and Tyrone knew each other and were enemies. So, I couldn't let either of them know I knew them. So, now I think I'm a playa. Not knowing deep inside that I was degrading myself. Naw, I'm a playa.

Well, one day I was standing in front of Tyrone house and Rob drove down the street and saw me hugging Tyrone. I couldn't explain my way out of that. I was busted. When Tyrone found out I knew Rob he stopped talking to me. After a whole lot of begging and pleading I got Rod to forgive me and talk back to me until the day I found out he had a baby on the way. One thing I didn't want was a baby. Gwen (my mother) told me all the time if I get pregnant she'd do the abortion. All of this happened before high school.

Once I got to high school it was a different level and my experiences never got better. Yes I had boyfriends then, still thinking I'm a playa. I had to have the popular boys though. Freshman year it was 2 football players the first half of the school year. One of them wanted to be a playa as well and caused me to fight another girl over him. So that ended that.

The second half of freshman's year the guy I dated was a junior. Fine as wine. Juan was his name. He had pretty light brown eyes, butterscotch brown skin, and sexy smile with a solid gold tooth on the side. I was walking to class with my best friend and she asked, "Why do u wear skirts so much?" I said it's easy access for my man. From that day forward every time Juan saw me he'd tug on the side of my skirt. Then we exchanged numbers. I use to stay after school just to ride the activity bus and kiss Juan. We use to take the last seat in the back of the bus, cause it's always dark and we'd kiss and play touchy-feely. I was so scared to have sex for fear that it would get all around the school and I'd be talked about so, I wouldn't let it go too far.

However, during this era all the girls were letting their boyfriend put passion marks on their neck. So now I finally had a chance to have my boyfriend do this to me. (Not knowing what it really represented.) All I knew was all the popular girls or the girls in the in crowd had this and I wanted to be included. So Juan use to always keep a passion mark on me somewhere visible normally just on my neck or jaw. Well, Juan ended up leaving school so that ended us. Outta sight outta mind.

This reckless behavior I was active in was the biggest example of low self esteem. However, I didn't know it. Relationship after relationship I experienced negative behavior. I had one night stands not because I wanted to have them. It was because once I met someone, I'd pour my heart and soul out to them thinking they were really interested in me because I felt there was a connection. We would have sex. There were even times when I would talk on the phone for days, hours, or months and then I think, "Wow, he really likes me. I really have something here." I would invite him to my house (thinking we knew each other well enough). We'd have sex, then he was out the door then I'd never hear from him again.

I remember in my junior year of high school, I went to prom with this guy who didn't go to my school. My close friend Lavonda did my hair and she even gave me the dress to wear. What I didn't know was this was this guy literally didn't care for me and hurt me in the worst way possible. What I didn't know was I was his date and so was another girl. He even left me and went to the hotel with her because, he knew I wasn't gonna have sex with him. His mother paid for me to catch a cab home, cause I didn't have a way. This began the emotion in me that I'll never be enough for anyone. During this time of all this ridiculousness I was attending church. You see I said, "attending". My grandma raised me in church so I knew who God was however; I didn't have a relationship with him. Trust me it's important to have a relationship with God.

When I became an adult my life didn't change much because I was still wanting to be included, wanting to be loved, and be a part of the "in" crowd. As I just said I attended church. Well, during this time the midnight musicals use to be poppin. The popular young ladies at that time, in my eyes, the beautiful young ladies always went. I asked my grandma, "Can I go with them?" and she let me go. However, I had a curfew they didn't. They were dressed in the latest and greatest name brand clothes. I wasn't. So to me (in my eyes) I was the ugly duckling, just tagging along cause not one of the guys noticed me. I wasn't pretty enough in their eyes. So what do I do?? This led me to thinking I wasn't attractive to anyone. The guys in church weren't attracted to me. The guys out of church just wanted sex.

So I said forget it I'ma go in the military. I wanted to escape it all. I took the test and passed it. When it came time to take the physical I learned I was pregnant. What, pregnant??? No, this can't be right. I went to the emergency room because, I needed a second opinion. So I went to the ER and lied about my symptoms thinking I'd get a different outcome. The nurse said, "You sound pregnant." I took the test. I was. See at that time, yes I was sexually active, just to the wrong men. So, now I'm a single mother with one child and didn't know who his father was. I had to get in front of the church and ask for forgiveness, cause I had a child out of wedlock. I'm sure my grandmother hated the shame I brought to my family.

After this I slowed down and tried to remain in one relationship so this wouldn't happen again. So, I had friends. Well, that's what I thought they were because 3 yrs later I got pregnant again by my friend and now I have a daughter. I didn't want my daughter to be reckless like me, so I began to change how I dressed and changed my behavior with men. However, it wasn't the outside of me that needed changing it was the inner me. My soul was lost and I didn't know it.

As I began coming more to church, I began to want more of God. As I began to seek God, more layers of hurt began to fall off me. So when I met my younger son's father, I thought he was the one because his mother was an evangelist and he was raised in church. However, he was very manipulative and lied to me constantly. He asked me to marry him and I was head over heels, only to find out that he was already married to a woman and never divorced her. I got pregnant by him and had my youngest son, Kahiem thinking if I did everything right he'd stay with us. This was the hardest pregnancy I ever had. I was placed on bed rest for 5 months of the pregnancy due to many complications. After I delivered him the doctors asked me if I knew who God was. They told me the arteries in my placenta were like angel hair spaghetti noodles and at any time if they would have ruptured I would have bled to death. I thought with him knowing this that would make him not only care for his son, but care for me also. Nope, it didn't. Shortly after my son was born he left to be with another woman. This woman was bigger than me so of course this made me feel the lowest of the low.

Well, my friends asked me to go the club with them one night to help take my mind off the hurt and that's where I met Timothy (my husband). Our versions of how we met are different, however mine is the best version. This unattractive man with a turtleneck sweater was talking to me. I looked up and I saw this very attractive man with the prettiest brown eyes walking past me. He had on a tan and brown hat with the matching sweater and baby, he was so fine. I couldn't stop looking at him. I turned my head for one second and he was gone. Well, later that night he came up behind me and asked me, "Put your number in my phone." I did!!! Wellllllll ......We talked on the phone for a few weeks. One night he came over to my house to hang out. One thing led to another and I slept with him on the first night. After he left I felt so low. I beat myself up. I did it again. I asked myself, "Why do you keep doing this?"

Well, I just prepared myself to never hear from him again. However, he called again and we continued to hang out. We went through many obstacles throughout our relationship. A lot of the things we went through, a lot of women would have walked away. The main thing was being with him and the love I have for him. We were together for 10 years before we got married. At first he told me over and over that he'd never marry anyone. However, we married and to this day are still married.

To some degree I was battling things in my mind. So, I got with a group of women and we began to break down things about our lives. Talking about how a lot of my hurt stemmed from me being hurt from things in my childhood helped tremendously to better understand what I did and did not get from my parents. In order to begin healing I had to have some hard conversations with my parents. So I talked to my mom and she let me know when I was growing up she was a single mother doing the best she could. No one ever gave her the rules to raising children. She let me know she wanted me and she loved me. This same day I let me father know how he was the first example of how I was to be loved by a man and he dropped the ball. He began to tell me how things were when I was a baby. See, my dad had me his senior year to of high school at age 17. He didn't want to breakup with his high school sweetheart, so he kept me a secret until the secret could not longer be hidden. This really was a dagger in my heart. That day I chose to get closure to my pain on how I grew up, only added more pain and made my self esteem go even lower.

Even though I was married at this point in my life I still battled with low self esteem. It really took for me to have a desire to want more of God in my life in order for things to change. I came to church on a regular basis at this point however, I didn't just attend. I began to put action to the things the pastor spoke about. I prayed more and talked to God. I have been talking to God so much in my life now that I'm sure he saying, "Ok Lisa, I hear you."

One day I was at the mall with my son Kahiem and a song by Cyndi Lauper called, Girls Just Wanna Have Fun came on. I was singing and dancing to this oldie but, goodie. Kahiem looked at me and said to other people in the store, "I don't know this lady". I went home and listened to this song looked up the lyrics and sang it for 2 weeks. This was the happiest I ever was in my entire life. I felt nothing or no one could take this happiness from me. Well, I was wrong.

My son was murdered by his alleged best friend. This hurt worst than anything I've ever felt …Worst than being left by a man, worst than losing my mom, and worst than losing anything. I have totally had to lean on God. I have asked him many times, "Why me Lord ?" I've asked,"Is it for me to ever me happy?? Is it for me to be loved and love others?"

I loved my kids dearly cause they are the only people in this world I feel truly love me unconditionally. To experience pain through my entire life has been the norm for me. However, it's not what God has for me!!!! I'm learning you keep God first your destiny in life will manifest in your life. No one else can define who you are and no one else opinion matter about you. Not even your children. The more I let this sink in the better and better I feel about myself. There are times when I still have to kill that negative voice that comes around and say I can't do something or I'm not pretty enough or good enough. I then tell that voice, "Greater is He that is in me than he that is in the world." (**1 John 4:4**).

Be blessed.

Pauletta

Psalm 139:14
I will praise You, for I am fearfully and wonderfully made;
Marvelous are Your works, And that my soul knows very well.

When God Is With You

I will make it as short as I can; this is just a little part. It started when I was about 5 years old. I had a true soprano voice. I would use my voice at every opportunity, just running and screaming while I played. One day as I running, suddenly I felt these pops in my throat. My tonsils had ruptured. I was literally drowning in my blood. My grandma ran out of the house and at some point got a straw down my throat which saved my life as she got me to the hospital.

When I woke up in St. Mary's Hospital, a nurse and doctors were surrounding my bed asking me if I wanted some ice cream or jello. I chose ice cream. When I looked around my room, I saw this real pretty light-skinned who was my roommate (at that time adults and kids were roomed together). She was so kind to me. She would comb my hair into pretty braids, polish my nails, and lotion me up. Little did I know, it was my dad that she was after and she was the devil in disguise. Who knew?

My dad said this lady named Chyna, my roommate, would be taking care of me for a while. (My mom had been ripped from my life when I was 4 years old and institutionalized, but that's a whole other story.) My dad was tall, well dressed, handsome with thick wavy hair. He would come pretty regularly and they would turn on the color television, it had 2 colors; half red/half green that pulled down like a window shade. This was done to distract me, while they talked for what seemed to be hours. I still thought Chyna taking care of me was her being nice and caring. So, when I was told that she would be moving in with us at our new house on 5244 Cabanne, I thought she would be there until my mom got back. Wrong!

Right after the big move, things began to change rapidly. I began to notice she would do things for us to get dad's attention. She was very creative. We were never shown affection with hugs or kisses. Sometimes, we were lucky to get a pat on the head.

The abuse began with her telling lies on me. I was the middle child out of three girls and I looked like my mother's twin, which was a reminder to everyone. My dad began to change. He stopped coming home at night. Chyna would call all around searching for him. When she did get him, she would tell a bunch of barefaced lies on me about things that she alleged I had done. When he got off work from the post office, he would come home and beat me. He would be so exhausted afterward, that he would fall asleep immediately. It was guaranteed that he would be home that night. Later, Chyna would pull me to the side out of guilt and tell me that my daddy really loved me. Eventually though, her lying phone calls about me weren't working anymore, so Chyna upped her game.

I was also loved starved for any crumbs of affection. Chyna began to abuse me out of her frustration, because of her no longer getting dad's attention like it was in the beginning. I couldn't understand what I could have done to cause her sudden hatred of me. Eventually, it would come to a head, but I wouldn't know this until it was too late.

Chyna was busy around the house. She sweetly called, "Pauletta?" When I got to her, she laid a box into my seven year old hands. It was a box of matches. She looked at me, "Run downstairs and light the water tank." I was a people pleaser. I had never lit a water tank before, but Chyna told me to strike the match and stick it in the opening until it lights. What I didn't know is had previously she had gone in the basement and put the pilot light out which caused

36

gas build up. I went down to the basement and lay down on the floor directly in front of the little opening striking match after match. Around the seventh try, I struck the match and fire shot out like a blow torch. The flames caught my favorite red checked blouse on fire. I ran blindly up the stairs with my arm covering my face while my shirt burned in flames. It seemed like forever running up those steps. Once I got to the top, I ran toward the front door. Suddenly, I felt someone snatch me by my arm and throw me down in a rug or blanket and roll me up, putting out the fire. The fire was out, but my flesh was swollen, burned black, and smoking.

Suddenly, the front door flew open. It was my dad. How could he have known? I reached for him to console and comfort me, instead he was angry. "Shut up before I give you something to cry about." He began yelling, saying that he had to leave his job, because Chyna had told him I was downstairs playing with matches. He drove me to Homer Phillips Hospital in his yellow drop top, yelling and cussing all the way. When we pulled up, he was still cussing. The doctors and nurses thought I was in shock, because I was quiet. They knew I had to be in pain, because my burned skin was still smoking. Yes, I was in excruciating pain, but for fear of getting a beating there was no way I would cry.

Now, I know that God's plan was what got me to the hospital to protect me from the abuse. Homer G. Phillips became my resident home for a year and a month. I never saw Chyna or my dad. I had heard that he had come to sign for the surgeries that I would need. No one from my family came to visit that year, except my Popa (grandfather). He came about 5 different times after church on Sundays. He would bring me my favorite, chocolate ice cream. I began to make friends in the hospital. But my nurse, Ms. Orange, was different.

She was mean and dark in color. She had a tough demeanor,

but she was really not mean as time passed. She was there after my four different surgeries and skin grafts. She was always there to take care of me with the half body cast and my hygiene. After a few weeks had passed, she was the one who would assist in removing the cast that supported my arm. I was go happy to get it off! Little did I know what was next. I was being prepared for being lowered into a vat of saline salt solution. It was as if acid was on my skin, all I could do was scream and cry. This was guaranteed at least twice a week after each of the 4 surgeries. Next, they would apply a white cream and a layer of gauze on it for a week or two, only to be pulled off after my flesh had healed to it. They said that it was dead skin they were pulling off for the new skin to grow. Everyone in the hospital knew my agonizing cries and screams.

When I got back to my cubicle, other nurses and patients would bring me stuffed animals as a comfort to me. I was confused. I spent a lot of time blaming myself for what had happened. I felt like this was some sort of punishment. Then again I was taken to surgery. This time my cast was higher up on my left arm and was positioned high in the air. Ms. Orange would gently wake me up, so that she could tend to my cast and hygiene. The surgeon came for me after a couple of weeks, taking me back to the operating room where the saline vat was in place. He cut the cast off and lowered me into the solution of salt.

Ms. Orange came to my cubicle and asked me how I felt about going home. I told her that I would be so happy. Popa came that Sunday and told me that he would be picking me up that Monday or Tuesday. I imagined the big celebration they were planning for my home coming. Wrong! When Popa came to get me from the hospital, he and my grandmother had to find clothes, shoes, and underwear for me, because Chyna said she had got rid of them because I had outgrown them. I was just glad to go home no matter what the situation. Later, I got all new clothes and toys.

What I have learned from this moment in life is that I am not damaged goods. My scars are scars of survival and victory. I am one of God's miracles…you can't kill what God has anointed to live. Those that meant me harm are no longer with us and I have forgiven everyone that was involved living and deceased. Yes deceased, because that bitterness would have lived on had I held on to the unforgiveness. Thank God for being set free. Amen.

The Beautiful Ones

Tameya

2 Corinthians 5:7
For we walk by faith, not by sight.

The Impact of 24

I wasn't always the Woman you see today! I was a Classy, hood street chick straight from the bottom. All my life I had to fight for my place in this world literally! Fight for just being me, fight for not being who people wanted me to be, fight because I was just simply different and stood out. Back then I wasn't aware that it was actually a spiritual fight going on that got physical. So here goes a short piece of my story and I pray that my testimony blesses whoever reads it and changes your life to the Glory of GOD!

I was this young girl that had BIG dreams of doing ballet on stages, modeling, making my own clothing and owning my own fancy hair salon. I would travel all around the world and open upscale salons in various states. I had a made up mind that I was not having children before I accomplished all my dreams and was happily married. I had it all planned out to a T the way my life was going to go. Then I got dragged into the fast life that was in my environment everyday. Working hard wasn't getting it fast enough for me so I decided that I would sell drugs to help me get what I wanted.

Remember I said in the beginning I wasn't always the woman you see today. I was a girl trying to grow up before my time. I was determined to get mines and get out this hood that I hated so badly. As I can remember, I have always been about my business even as a kid. It got me noticed by those who were the bosses around my way. I was know as Lil Tameya the quiet, cute girl that dressed up all the time and be in her own lane! People said I was different from the

41

other girls; it was just something about me that was special. Me being so humble never really tripped off all the compliments people gave me, I was just being me. The more compliments the others heard people give me, the more hate I got and the more people wanted to fight me. Not wanting people to think I was a punk I would call people out or fight whoever wanted to fight me. Most of the time it was more than one person, so I was getting jumped which caused my mother to get involved and my little brother, Frank. Frank would always tell me to not trust people around that way because they hate on me so hard, but I still had to give people a chance.

Those so called friends were a lot of the reasons why I was fighting and getting jumped on and why I became what we called: THE BEAST! Angry about all the betrayal and tired of kicking down doors, fighting breaking my fingers and getting my hair pulled out, I decided I would make my haters even madder and shine harder on them. I know none of them were actually capable of touching me and my hustle on their best day, so I turned my swag on a thousand! So I felt like if they wanted to talk about me, let me give them something to talk about. Tameya went to "MaMa Meya" mode is what I called it and that was ugly.

I began to not care about what people had to say, I was determined to get it by any means necessary. I kept two jobs, but I sold drugs on the side. The fast life was getting excited to me! All the money I was making allowed me to triple my wardrobe, I always had a lot of nice stuff because of my parents, but this was all my doing!

I had a fetish for cars with big rims, candy paint, loud beats & TVs. With the money I was having I was able to switch cars like I changed clothes which was a lot. The clothes I put on became less and the jewelry got bigger with more sparkles. My mom would be so scared for me, but I felt like I was untouchable. My popularity went through the roof because I was out clubbing every night in the limelight. Plus I always carry extra protection on me for my hatters. Deep down inside, I guess, I was praying I would never have to use it! The hood life had me in a trance. I was stuck in a zone never I'd imagined being in trying to get out! I wasn't hanging in my hood as I grew it was the actual opposite. I hung in other neighborhoods with the fellas who were bossed up that showed me more love than my neighborhood ever had.

Don't get me wrong I still had a lot of love from the O.G.'s & others from my way, so if you weren't them you couldn't be in my space! My attitude became the worst to people I disliked and the gangster in me was heading me down the wrong road. I didn't realize that a spirit had jumped into me and was on a straight mission. But, someone had to be praying for me because of all the danger I was putting myself in! I was running around like a dude chasing cash, clubbing late night by myself, smoking weed, showing out to make my hatters mad. It could have gotten me killed or in jail, But, I was safe & covered from the unseen. Not to mention all the guys I had thinking I was a pimp and had my nerve to think it was cute. Using them for their money, because I got bored, keeping one for ever financial thing I needed to do, never catch feelings, and not upping the goods unless I saw the potential of keeping him. I didn't allow them to know the real me. My mentality was *I'm going do it to them before they do it to me.* So I played hard and stayed hard, plus they like it.

All that anger was built up on men, because I was hurt from my 1st love. At a young age, I had no business trying to have a boyfriend anyway that was way older than me. Plus, my dad wasn't around and stepfather was going away as well. I just felt if I love them they would eventually bail so why bother!

My other family was in church and had a relationship with

GOD, but I was never interested. My mother wasn't in church and she never made us go. Frank and I would have a hunger to go sometimes on our own when we were little, but never knew why. I remember we use to play in door of the church down the street from us every evening. I mean they were having a Holy Ghost straight up party (now that I know better). One day they were waiting on us when we did it again. Lol! I remember feeling bad, the lady was really nice and she told us we were welcome to come in and we didn't have to be scared to come inside. So we came in for a second, but left shortly when they started shouting young and ignorant to the fact of what was taking place.

At the age 20 I began to work for my cousin, Honey's, hair salon as her assistant. This is where my thirst for my childhood dreams came back. Reality began to sit in that I needed to change and had gotten far off track from who I use to be. Working for her I was forced to stay out the clubs as much because my schedule there intervened. My schedule was Thursday, Friday and Saturday from 7:45am to sometimes 2AM. I would be wore out, but I was determined, never was late or missed a day for 3 years until my last day. I learned a lot there about the salon business and cosmetology. So in the summer of 2008 I enrolled in Vatterot Cosmetology School in Berkeley, St. Louis. The excitement was real!

I still was in the streets due to having rent & bills plus no job was willing to work with my school schedule. I was applying for everywhere, the crazy part is I would get hired, but it would clash with my school schedule. I was determined to learn everything I could, so the focus was completely on school. Which meant the hustle in the street was slowing down. In class I met a lady name Christy. She was older than me and kept to herself like I did. We began to chat here and there in class on projects and eventually started eating lunch together.

She was good at certain things I wasn't and I was good at certain things she wasn't. So we decided to teach each other. Not knowing it was a setup by GOD. We became extremely close like sisters by the end of second phase. She would always invite me to events her family had, but I would never come (still having trust issues from the past). I finally came over one day after class and met her mom! OMG, you talking about an angel in human form I call her. Mother Hemphill and the family treated me as family from the 1st day we met. They would invite me to church every week, but I never came.

In the mist of all this, I hadn't noticed that I wasn't in the streets at all. I was holding drugs & I wasn't selling. I began to get this feeling inside of me that I couldn't shake! It had a hold on me like no other and it was extremely strong! One day in January 2009 turning 24 life was getting different and serious. I heard a voice calling me! I thought it was Victoria my brother, Frank's girlfriend, playing a trick on me it was so loud and clear. To the point we started arguing, because I got mad thinking she was lying saying she was not calling my name and was playing with me.

One Sunday morning I left my key in Christy car & she was at Emmanuel Temple, so I had to come to church to get it she said. Lol. I remember not wanting to come, because I smelled like weed that I was smoking and I wasn't dressed appropriately. But, I had no choice if I wanted to get in my house. Now I as I think back I call it THE SETUP! I had no idea it was Family and Friends Day at the church that Sunday. I remember walking in and everyone was extremely nice, it was overwhelming with getting love, hugs and smiles like they knew me. When I met the pastor, he introduced himself and asked my name I told him Tameya and that I was Christy's friend. He was very different and humble from other pastors I had met that made me not interested in GOD.

45

When I left that day a sudden feeling came over me that I never felt before. I remember a voice telling me to drop the drugs and give everything away and I'll be forever blessed. I thought I was going crazy hearing this voice in my head. The same voice that was calling my name and that was in my dreams I had been having that had been telling me to run, jump, turn, go straight. It was really weird to me.

I promise Mother Hemphill and the family I would come back to visit church, so in April 2009 I did. That day changed my life! The moment I walked in the door it felt right, then I was shocked with something so simple but important enough to me GOD used it to draw me forever. Pastor Whittier walked up to me and said full of joy and excitement "Sister Tameya! I been asking about you and praying for you." That got away with me! For him to remember my name after only meeting me one time for a few seconds. My name is not a common name to remember and to actually pronounce it correctly. This simple thing changed my life!

I walked in Emmanuel Temple Church that day heard the word GOD needed me to hear about FAITH, I joined and never turned back! When you say I went cold turkey on everything that wasn't GOD! Please believe it! I was so serious I thought I was going to die or get killed; it was to good of a feeling to be true. I was on a high like no weed could ever give me! My so called friends said I had lost my mind giving away all them drugs, money, and not having sex. They said I would be back at it, I was just going through something and needed to snap out of it so we could get this money. But, I was dead serious it was over for me.

Then I heard the voice say remove yourself from people, places and things even your mother. Now that was hard. I cried because, I didn't understand but something inside of me knew I had to listen. Then the voice told me to "talk to them all, some will

46

understand and some won't. Those who won't can't go with you where you're going anyway! It will hurt from the ones you least expect BUT I'll give you strength to endure it all! You gone to lose some friends, but I'll give you new friends that will grow with you."

I pushed away from my best friend/ mother for 30 days only called her on the phone to check on her and popped up once a week to see her face. All I would talk about is church and GOD I was shining in a new way! Not knowing everyone could see it that I came in contact with. I began to take Faith at its challenge and GOD was leading me.

My mom saw the change and decided she would finally except my offer and visit my church. You talking about exited I was lit! Lol! Not only her, my sister wanted to come, and some friends. They said if GOD can change you I need to give Him a try. In May 2009 we got baptized and received the gift of the Holy Ghost in a tarrying service at the old church. This was life changing for me and everyone in my life. I can't explain the feeling; you just gotta experience it for a lifetime! Days later the whole entire crew I was running with in the street went down in a big drug cartel bust! I was so glad GOD spared me and saw me fit to grab me up out of it all!

The next week we had a task at school to find a salon to work in as a grade, but I couldn't find it in me to do the project. My teacher keep threatening to write me up, knowing she had a job to do I would tell her do what she gotta do, because I'm not gone waste my time or theirs doing it because I'm gone have my own salon. She was like, *Girl, don't do that, I had a salon it's terrible. It's hard, go work in somebody else's shop and pay booth rent it's easier.*

My 1st phase teach Mrs. Keke over heard it one day and was upset. She called me into the hall and asked me have I ever heard of walking by Faith & not by sight? I was like "No!" She began to

47

break it down for me. Then she said "Stop telling them your plans, because some people can speak negative over your life before you get a chance to grow in it." Then before she walked off she turned around and said "Speak things into existence. Whatever you want say it like you already got it! But, keep GOD 1st." I always liked her and was glad she was my 1st teacher in cosmetology. Mrs. KeKe helped me stick through it when I wanted to give up and go work. She would always encourage us and her swag reminded me of myself, but on another level. Plus, she was 2 years younger than me and I respected how she carried herself in there with messy women.

Anyway back to the testimony, leaving Bible study one evening dropping off Sister Ann, I got lost trying to get back to the highway. I mean, I could see it but, couldn't remember how to get to it. I began to get nervous, because I was in Walnut Park and it was getting dark and I'm lost. The third time around I was going slow to call for help on my phone and GOD said look to the left! I saw a building with a sign saying beauty salon for rent. I accidentally called it trying to save it in my phone. The lady called back and we began to talk I told her my story. She was blow away with it and how young I was she said it was something about me she was excited to meet. Then she began to say how much she wanted for rent which was $1,000.00 a month, with 1st, last month rent and security deposit which added up to $3,500.00. Now mind you, I was broke, struggling to pay rent at my house and bills while trying to graduate. I didn't want to waste her time, because she had others who had the money that wanted it. So I told her I didn't have it and how GOD told me give everything away and he will provide. She said for me to see what I can do in a week and once she returned from her trip she would call me.

I was so excited I started praying to GOD, then I called my mother telling her and my friends. Everyone was excited and said let us know what we need to do. Sitting in class GOD finally spoke,

"Have a car wash!" I'm like a car wash? I don't wash cars! I'm still with that "pretty gurl" mentality and too good to wash a car outside. He said again "Have a car wash!" At the time I lived in North County and everyone I knew stayed in the city, so I knew they weren't coming out my way. So I asked my mom if I could do it at her house since she still was in the old neighborhood. I knew the love I had would out shine those who hated me.

Saturday morning me and my girls got up early gathering everything we needed headed to my mom's house. My mom and siblings sold waters and snacks while the car wash took place on her front. Within 30 minutes I had the entire neighborhood lined up outside to support! Some didn't even get a car wash they just donated hundreds of dollars, just because they said they always knew I was going to be something great when I grew up. Out of all the cars that was washed GOD spoke to me and said "Look, you never washed one."

All my friends were washing them. They kept telling me to move, just collect the money. See GOD never said I had to wash the cars HE just said have a car wash. Here I was debating with GOD at first and He never had me to do something I didn't want to do. But, I was willing to even if it was out of my element. Test number two, I passed it! When the lady got back she called! I was so excited I told her I wanted it. She started laughing and said but you haven't even seen it yet. My response was I don't care, I feel inside I'm gone love it, so when can we meet? She was blown away that I made all that money in a day she said, "Girl, I gotta meet you, can you come tomorrow?" We agreed upon a time to meet the next day and hung up.

The next morning I went to the bank to get the cashiers check, then pulled up with my family to the building. She smiled excited to meet me; it was like we met before and the connection was sweet. I walked in and was amazed by the inside as I knew I would be. As I walked around look at the setup, it had 5 stations, 2 shampoo bowls, 4 hair dryers with chairs, 8 waiting area chairs, and a room off to the side with a glass display case filled with hair supplies, a cash register, mini refrigerator, microwave, and shelves on the wall with more supplies.

Then down the stairs was a barbershop with 2 barber stations, a break room, a restroom, a storage area and a small spot with a pinball machine that was filled with change. I was beginning to realize I had all the money for her, but I would need my own equipment, supplies, and etc with no money. I began to speak it out loud not even realizing it, but what came out her mouth blew me away! The lady said "You can have everything that is in there, including the money." I began praising GOD! You talking about a blessing! I was completely out done!

The next day I went to school and started recruiting some people I had been watching that was clocking out that week with clientele already to come work at my salon. They were very excited to work with me and even more excited that I was only 24 years old handling my business. I set a date to meet them there that Friday so they could see if they like it and would like to work in the area since it was in the city. But, it was the only salon in the area so that was a plus. On Friday they all came and loved it! We did a lease agreement for $100 a week booth rental for 1 year and everyone setup that day and we planned strategies to open that place with nothing but success that blew my mind. I mean they were on it! We all were all on one accord.

I still had a few weeks before I could clock out, so I would go in between school. Talking to my class about what GOD had done and that we had a grand opening the next week, another young lady walked up to me asked me to ride with her it was important. I was nervous at 1st, because I was so to myself but I took a ride curious about what she wanted really. She end up telling me her mom was killed by her husband and left her everything. It was really sad to hear her story because she was only 22 years old, but had an old soul. She really knew what she wanted out of life and was an extremely smart young lady. She said that she had been watching me and over heard me telling my story about how I was trying to stay on the right path and out the streets and was on a mission to open my own business. It kept being on her heart to bless me. Not realizing we had pulled up to a bank, we had spent the entire time just testifying to each other about our lives. She told me she would be right back. She got out the car went inside the bank, then came and handed me a $900.00 check then said get whatever you want for your business with this. I started to cry instantly! I said, "OMG, I can't take this Love!" She told me don't knock her blessings and learn how to receive one when it's given to you. I hugged her so tight and thanked her with tears falling down my face. Not only that she pulled the up to the beauty supply and spent $600 on gallons of products, towels etc. to help! She called it her grand opening gift. Lol!

On grand opening day I was extremely excited. All my family, friends and church family was there to support. The community showed so much love and respect to me, someone anonymously called the news and radio station to come out, because they felt like it was awesome to see. We had music, barbecue on the grill, all our hair mannequins were outside on the fence for display, a car wash was taking place, spa services, raffles, and not to mention the decorations was gorgeous. As I stood there counting the thousands of dollars I made at the end of that week. GOD spoke to me and said "I told I got you! Now if you take care of my house I'll take care of yours!" I paid my tithing that Sunday and He gave it right back that Tuesday when we opened up! That's where my FAITH IN GOD got deeper.

The Beautiful Ones

I opened May 1, 2009; 19 days before my best friend/little brother, Frank Session A.K.A Nitty, came home from spending 6 years in jail. His story is another story in my life's book I'll write later. But, anyway he was so proud of his sister that he was bragging to everyone he talked to. Lol! I would hear him on the phone telling people, "I'm staying with my sister, man, she doing her thang! She got her own big 4 bedroom house, 2 full baths, I got the top floor." Lol! "Yep, she just opened her own salon and got her car fixed up nice, she jamming no kids or dude to be eating off her success". This month was very exciting for me, because I received the Holy Ghost which I prayed so hard to receive & it finally happened! Hallelujah!

Things were going all so well, it's like I was dreaming. Then my life was completely changed on August 28, 2009 at 11:57pm. I got a call from my mother screaming that my little brother was killed. I was so angry! I yelled at GOD, crying so hard asking why He let this happen to me and I changed my life for Him. I was disappointed, hurt, confused and mad! I wanted revenge and bad. Then GOD spoke to me the next morning as I stepped out to find them. I began to quote scripture out loud that I never knew I knew, screaming them on my mom's porch. GOD told me to let vengeance be His!

That was the hardest test I would ever have to take in this life. See the enemy wanted me to go back to my old ways. He wanted to make me and everything I was standing for a lie. That was my JOB moment (**JOB 2;3**) see no matter how he tried to come at me, GOD knew me! GOD knew I loved my brother and would kill for him, But, He knew I loved Him much more! So, I fought against the spirit that was trying to get to my flesh. I got grounded even more in the Word of GOD! I prayed harder! I worked harder like never before to keep me from being idol. I stayed in the House of GOD every day the door was open. The more I spent time with GOD the more in love I became and the less anger I felt and the more He blessed me.

GOD started giving me deeper dreams & visions. I had them since I was a kid, but never knew it was a gift. I learned more about my gifts & talents then began to use them. My dreams became more clear, I mean I could remember every single detail. I began to seek guidance from my 1st Lady & Pastor. They would tell me to write them down and watch them manifest themselves in my life. Over the years I start walking in the visions GOD gave me. He told me **NO GOOD THING WOULD HE WITHHOLD FROM ME IF I CONTINUE TO WALK UPRIGHT BEFORE HIM!**

GOD promised me if I take care His house that He would take care of my house. And if I take care His business, He would take care of my business. GOD has not let me down. Even when the enemy tried to come up against me and it set me back by killing my brother, then losing my grandmother 2012, whole house getting robbed 2013, 2016 contractors running off with my money, trying to destroy my building GOD told me to get in 2017 and losing my daughter 8/18/17. I know GOD allowed all of it to bless me even the more and so HE can be Glorified!

So I have grown to always say, "Praise GOD any how!" and really mean that. See, I know just like GOD had JOB go through all those hard moments in life, didn't mean He didn't love him. It was actually the opposite. He knew no matter what obstacles the enemy would try to bring his way Job would not let go his love for GOD. He would remain faithful. So if you know me or talk to me, my conversations and responses are different from most. I feel like a superhero/untouchable with GOD on my side!

I'm fearless now, I look at life totally different, so I embrace and enjoy every single moment with those I love. My faith is unrealistic to a lot of people BUT it's all I know. Without my faith in GOD I wouldn't be me. I'm so at peace in GOD and all He has established through me, because I'm only the overseer because, all I have belongs to GOD. He just let me borrow it all and I promised to be Faithful to all of it!

Thanks for listening to just a short piece of my life. I pray that this would be a great impact on your life and would change your world along with taking your faith in GOD to another level. GOD Bless you with 24 Things To Remember & 1 Thing To Never Forget.

Love always Tameya Bank

24 Things To Remember And One Thing To Never Forget

1. Your presence is a present to the world.
2. You're unique and one of a kind.
3. Your life can be what you want it to be.
4. Take the day just one at a time.
5. Count your blessings, not your troubles.
6. You'll make it through whatever comes along.
7. Within you are so many answers.
8. Understand, have courage, be strong.
9. Don't put limits on yourself.
10. So many dreams are waiting to be realized.
11. Decisions are too important to leave to chance.
12. Reach for your peak, your goal, your prize.
13. Nothing wastes more energy than worrying.
14. The longer one carries a problem, the heavier it gets.
15. Don't take things too seriously.
16. Live a life of serenity, not a life of regrets.
17. Remember that a little love goes a long way.
18. Remember that a lot... goes forever.
19. Remember that friendship is a wise investment.
20. Life's treasures are people... together.
21. Realize that it's never too late.
22. Do ordinary things in an extraordinary way.
23. Have health and hope and happiness.
24. Take the time to wish upon a star.

1. And don't ever forget...For even a day...Just how much I do really love you. –Written by: Frank Session

The Beautiful Ones

Ann

1 Peter 2:9
You are a chosen race, a royal priesthood, a holy nation, a peculiar people, that ye should show forth the praises of Him who hath called you out of darkness into His marvelous light.

CALLED ME OUT OF DARKNESS INTO HIS MARVELOUS LIGHT

Hi! I would like to introduce myself, my name is Ann Bush-Curry. I'm a wife and mother of four adult children. God saved me at the age of 35. I thank the Lord for sending someone in my path to tell me boldly that I needed to repent. Now, I'm at the laundry mat early in the morning, I'm looking around seeing who she's talking too. I wait for a few minutes and went to see what this woman mean, I needed to repent. I didn't have a relationship with the Father, so I didn't know what she meant by that. I went outside didn't see this woman at all, she was dress like she was homeless, I can't say she was homeless, but I thank God for her obedience, allowing God to use her to draw me to him.

For God so love the world He gave His only begotten Son, whosoever believeth in Him should not perish, but have everlasting life
John 3:16

For God sent his Son into the world to condemn the world, but that the world through him might be saved
John 3:17

The Lord deliver me, he can deliver anyone, he delivers me from drinking, smoking marijuana, cussing, spirit anger, bitterness, resentment, spirit hatred and a spirit of fear. The Lord called me out of darkness into his marvelous light (**1 Peter 2:9**). Thank you Jesus for giving me a mind to be save! Glory Hallelujah!

Trust me, I don't have it all together, he's still working on me every single day. Sometimes we want to be delivered right there, but it can be a process. I had to remember all the years out there doing my own thing it takes some time. I thank God for being baptized in Jesus' name and filled with gift of the Holy Ghost!! The Holy Ghost is real that's the Spirit of GOD. He can keep us if we want to be kept. I don't have no desire to go backwards, but only going forward in him. I have been through so many trials and test, but I'm still here, if I didn't have a relationship with the Lord, I don't know where would I be right about now.

God is so real, He's a healer, a deliver, He healed my son from asthma, every day I had to go to the hospital, his asthma was so bad. I got so tired going to the hospital it seemed like I was going every week. I told myself, I'm going to stretch out my hand and pray and believing God is going to heal him. Believe it or not, God did heal Him from asthma, no more breathing treatment he was young at the time. I can go on and on, we just have to trust God and his Son Jesus, no matter what we're facing in this life. God will see us through, He said it in His word He will never leave us nor forsake us. I thank God we can to him in prayer, yes you can go to Him, and He's no respecter of a person. God bless you all.

Cynthia

Isaiah 26:3
Thou wilt keep him in perfect peace, whose mind
is stayed on thee.

GOD IS IN CONTROL

My life journey started in the city of Pine Bluff, Arkansas; where I was born and raised in a small family setting consisting of my sister; the oldest, me; the middle child, and my brother the youngest. My loving and caring mother moved to Milwaukee, Wisconsin after she had my bother with the mindset of "I now have three kids to take care of." (I need to make more money.) So I was raised by my grandmother.

My grandmother's sister took my sister and brother to her house to raise. From the age of 7 to 18 years, my life consisted of going to elementary, junior high, and then high school Monday thru Friday. I loved going to the school. I never wanted to miss a day. While attending school, I participated in different activities like singing in varsity choir, member of a modern dance group and on the pep squad. I confessed my life to Christ at the age of 14 and was baptized in a Baptist church. I was a member of the choir, and we had choir rehearsal on Saturdays. My sister and I thought we loved it and just had to have a piano. We had a paper route with regular customers. The route started on Thursday evenings until Saturday. We were told, if you want a piano you will have to save your money we earned from the paper route. After we had saved a certain amount we would be able to purchase a brand new piano. Then of course we had to take piano lessons. Our teacher's name was Professor Zachary; my sister did not like him. Because, he would tap your fingers with a long skinny stick which I think it is called a conductor's baton, whenever you hit a wrong key on the piano. I was hitting wrong notes, but the older people kept on singing and they didn't let me go. After we completed our lessons my sister stopped playing the piano. But, I kept playing and I was asked to play for my Sunday school and BTU, which started on Sunday evenings. I didn't really like it because I didn't think I could play the piano that good. But, most of all, I didn't like the fact that BTU which stands for Baptist Training Union, started at 6:00pm on Sunday evenings. And some of my friends would be going to movies on Sunday evenings and I couldn't go.

After I graduated from high school, I attended college, which was located behind my house for one year. While going to college I moved from home and started staying with my boyfriend. My first love, my boo thang, my everything, my one and only, so I thought. He was from East St. Louis, Illinois, which would explain how I ended up being in St. Louis, MO today. That's when things started changing for me for all the wrong reasons. But, I thought I was living the life. I stopped going to church.

Now, I'm thinking yeah, this is the life, not under my grandmother's roof. I can do whatever I want and whenever I want. I can come and go whenever I want. I started drinking alcohol, smoking cigarettes and drugs. My boyfriend and I had stopped going to our classes. We just wanted to party all the time. After the first year of college was over, I moved to Milwaukee, Wisconsin where my mother was living. My boyfriend moved back home to East St. Louis, IL. He came to visit me in Milwaukee, but I told him I didn't like how cold and how much snow they have in Milwaukee. So, we both decided that I would move to East St. Louis. I got a job working downtown in St. Louis. My boyfriend was working at the radio station. He also had a side job working illegally.

We were living the life. We had plenty of money and lived a luxurious life with him as he worked at a radio station. We were meeting and partying with different musicians and famous singers like Marvin Gaye, Stevie Wonder, the GAP Band, Bootsy Collins with the Parliament Funkadelic, and many others. He also had a sister that lived in California and she worked for Universal Studios in California. So we got to see the making of different movies and TV shows and also got to meet a few actors and actresses. But, living that lifestyle could be and was scary at times. But, to me at that time having the luxuries of life out weighed the scary times. I was going to vacation in the United States and out of the country, driving luxury cars, having lots of clothes, shoes, and jewelry. But, deep down inside, I wasn't happy. It was like something was missing in my life.

I broke up with my boyfriend and moved to St. Louis, because I was still working everyday in St. Louis. I dated a few guys after I got over my first love. I met my first husband. But, that marriage didn't last over a year. It was just something to do because I was over 30 and never had been married and had no kids. I was planning to move back to Milwaukee with my mother. Then, I started praying. I mean really praying like I had never prayed before. Asking the Lord to forgive me and help me, because I didn't want to keep living the life style I was living.

One day while I was at the hospital for blood work. I met my second husband. While we were dating we talked about going to church and God. We actually went to a few churches on Sunday were we knew some of the members. Then he told me about a mother and father that started a church and that he went to school with some of their children. That church is called Emmanuel Temple Church of God. He said, "It's not a Baptist church, but I know you will like it here."

We both joined Emmanuel Temple and got married at Emmanuel Temple. Although, my husband is deceased now I just know God put him in my life for a reason. I believe that reason was to bring me to Emmanuel Temple. I thank GOD everyday for keeping me while I was out in this world in my mess. I thank GOD for saving me and delivering me.

Isaiah 26:3
Thou wilt keep him in perfect peace, whose mind is stayed on thee.

You don't have to be embarrassed, ashamed, nor afraid to come back to GOD. Because, GOD is still GOD. Even if you have never been taught anything about GOD, just know that GOD is love: **1 John 4:16.** GOD lovesYou: **Isaiah 41:10**, GOD is in Control! **Psalm 46:1**, May GOD BLESS YOU!

Love, Peace, Happiness,
Cynthia Roberts

Stacey

Hosea 2:19

And I will betroth thee unto me for ever; yea, I will betroth unto me in righteousness, and in judgment, and in lovingkindness, and in mercies.

HEALED HURT WHOLE

I was nine years old when my father died at the age of 33. There are only 2 things I remember about his funeral. One was sitting in the backseat of the limousine, comforting my mother as best I could telling her I was going to take care of her, then remembering playing wiffle ball in the backyard with my cousins during the repast at our house. I don't remember crying. No one even mentioned my father after that day. So it didn't seem like it was something worth crying over. He was here. Now he was gone. Life would on. I would only find out years later he was shot playing Russian roulette with his best friend when they were high on drugs. His best friend dumped him at the ER entrance and left.

My mother said, she and my father met in high school. My father persistently asked her out. She said he was in a "special class" for troubled kids and she wasn't interested. He still persisted, but what changed things was when he stood up for her in front of her grandmother. My grandmother had a vicious tongue at times and a commanding presence. After my father refused to back down and my mom's heart changed. She wanted to escape the child abuse she was going through at home and my father had gained hero status in her eyes.

My father had a one problem, he was addicted to alcohol, so was my mother's father. When discovered at the age of 19, she was pregnant with me, she gave him an ultimatum. He had to give up the drinking or she'd leave him. He did. They got married and started their life together. But, it wasn't the happily ever after she had hoped for. He'd stopped drinking and moved on to taking drugs and selling drugs. While Mama worked full time at the postal service, she spent the early years trying to build a home for us. Between raising me and working, she was going back and forth to court for my father. She was only twenty years old and would be in that cycle for the next several years, trying to juggle our lives as a family.

The earliest memories of my mom consisted of me watching her get ready to go to work. She'd be dressed in her uniform and walk out the door with a large brown paper bag with her lunch in it. Once she was out the door, my time was spent between my great grandmother's house and my other grandmother (she wasn't actually related to us, but had played an instrumental part of my mother and aunts' lives, so that became her designation). When Mama was off on the weekend, she'd throw on some Al Green and I knew it was time to clean up, but once we cleaned up I'd spend all my time with her.

My father on the other hand was in and out of prison. My mother never complained about the hour and a half trip to see him. She never said a harsh work about him, so I never thought about why he was there. We'd drive from St. Louis to Illinois, park in a huge parking lot and go to this small brick building to get checked in. I wasn't even tall enough to reach the counter. I'd have to walk through x-ray machine. There was a large court yard area before we'd get to a large building that looked like a castle with iron bars. We'd be in the waiting room for hours. Eventually, it would be our turn to see him. We'd be navigated through a series of bars and that's all I remembered. I have pictures of him holding me while he was in prison and even have a couple of letters he wrote me, but I don't remember ever seeing him in jail. I was just looking forward to him coming home.

In my mind, I thought when he came home from prison he was going to pick me up in his arms and never let me go just like he wrote to me in his letters. But, it didn't happen that way. My mother tried to integrate him back into family life whenever he got out. One time, he had gotten a job at Carter Carburetor. Mom would drop him off in the morning and pick him up in the afternoon. But, things fell apart quickly. She found out by the 2nd or 3rd week that my father would walk into the building, then go out a side door and have one of his crew pick him up.

She still tried to honor his position as my father. She even let him pick me up from school. Then one day, when my mother and I were driving through a neighbor I pointed out a house my father had taken me and his best friend to the last time he had picked me up from school. I told her how daddy and his best friend had shotguns and kicked the door in and ransacked the house looking for something while I sat at the top of the stairs. A little girl had come home from school and when she saw what was happening, she was about to run away, but I convinced her that it was going to be alright, because my father was there and she'd be safe. That was the last time my mother let my father take me anywhere. But, that wasn't going to keep our family out of danger.

On my 9th birthday, I got a Charlie's Angels Kelly doll. I was so excited, I playing with her until I fell asleep. The next morning, my mother quietly opened the door that separated her bedroom from my bedroom. She whispered to me put my house shoes on and follow her. She gripped my hand, but I pulled against it, stretching out my hand toward the bed, "My doll." Mama didn't say anything on to great grandmother's house. She told me before she left, she'd be back. She was and before I knew it, we were headed to California. Mama went back home after about two weeks, then she sent for me 3 weeks later. Mama never said why we left. But not long after, I was interviewed by a case worker to see which parent I wanted to live with. My father had faltered in his promise to my mother to get clean, but she didn't falter in getting a divorce. Nine months later he was dead.

The lost of my father left me feeling vulnerable in a way I didn't understand. I loved him. As time when on my mother began to tell me about my father's dealings in the street. I felt it was my duty to protect his memory. So I built a web of memories that would paint him in a favorable light and put the other painful ones away, like the reason my mother had taken us to California. It would take a year before my mother would tell me the story.

My mother had a stroke from the stress of what my father was taking her through. She had gone to the doctor and he had given her a shot for her nerves. My father called her and once the medicine had taken effect he came home and confronted her about her riding with a co-worker to work. In a drug infused rage, he beat her all night and tried to make her hold a knife so he could, "kill her in self-defense". He said he was going to kill her, me, our dog, and even the fish in our aquarium tank. But, God intervened. He got tired and made my mother lay down with him. He wrapped his arms and legs around her, so he'd wake up if she moved, but she ended up rocking him to sleep. She said when she had gotten out of his arms, he was in an unconscious state. She got a marker, felt for his heart, and circled it, then picked up the knife. She said she heard a voice say, "No! I'll fight your battles." That's when she came and got me and we escaped. That was the first time I ever heard about God personally being interested in helping you, it wasn't what I understood about God.

My great grandmother was the one who took me to church. She'd sit me between her and my great grandfather. I seldom understood what the pastor was talking about, but I knew it must have been important, because my grandparents went to church every

Sunday and never missed. After my father died, my grandmother would talk to me about God. She was to the point. "You need to get baptized or you're going to go to Hell." It worked.

I got baptized at the age of 10. But, nothing changed in my life. I still held onto to the pain of losing my father. I had started believing the lie that I didn't mean enough to my father for him to give up his drugs and lifestyle. I was unloved and rejected. It led me into a chronic insecurity that was rooted in fear and showed up in my life as shame, guilt, and anger. I couldn't talk to anyone, because to be vulnerable was to be weak. It was a mindset I brought to God. I didn't know that I could have a real relationship with Him where I could talk to him about my pain and give Him the opportunity to heal it. Because of the early loss of my father, I was overly protective of the few close relationships I had. I wasn't just responsible for myself, but for the people I loved. I wasn't going to let anyone hurt them.

There was always a longing in my heart to get closer to God, but I'd go in and out of church trying to stay within the invisible boundaries I had set to keep me safe from God hurting me. My mind was messed up. I was afraid to get close to people, because I thought if they really knew how I was inside, I'd be rejected. When it came to men, I feared them. So if they showed any sign of weakness, I'd verbally attack them to make sure they didn't hurt me first. I spent the majority of my time single, but secretly longed for a healthy relationship I could feel safe in. But, my patterns said differently.

The first two men I ever came involved with were just like my father, emotionally unavailable, addicts, and by the second relationship heading for violence. I was drawn to them, because I felt like if I could heal them and save them, I'd accomplish the one thing that I couldn't with my father. I'd get them to love me, then I'd have value. Yet during that whole time, God was with me, using situations to draw me closer to Him, so He could truly show me that He is love. His love is unconditional, patient, and healing.

As God was drawing me closer, He filled me with the Holy Ghost, His very Spirit living within me. I had never felt so safe, yet vulnerable at the same time. There was always in the background my father's memory. The more I discovered about what love truly is, I realized that what I had protected in my father's memory wasn't love. I didn't know how to process the pain and anger felt toward him for what he had put me and my mother through. I still felt guilty about what he had done to other people's lives. I felt shamed about to talk to God about it, so I didn't. I lived in quiet desperation to be affirmed by a father figure. That decision led me into a relationship with a man who was 20 years my senior, emotionally and physically abusive. I was deeply involved in church, but I felt trapped in my own pain and shame to ask anyone how to get out of the relationship. I lived with the constant fear of hearing, "You should have known better.", "It's your fault." "You deserve it, because you got yourself into this."

Honestly, when God rescued me from that relationship, I did hear some of those things. It tore me to the core of my being, but in the midst of my pain God was there with me in a way that I never thought He would have ever been. He saw me for who I was. He saw the pain that my heart was in and helped me through it when I couldn't help myself. God did for me everything I would have wanted my father to do. He comforted me. He was there was for me when I cried. He told me the truth when I needed to hear it and protected me.

After I had broken off my last relationship and left the job where we had worked together, the man who abused me got arrested. He was facing some serious charges. Even though, I didn't want to be with him anymore, I found myself feeling sorry for him. What he

68

had done to me was horrible, but I knew because of the type of person he was, what he was going through was way worse, because it touched every area of his life, freedom, and reputation. I remember I was struggling with it in my mind one day as I was opening the door to go into the lobby of my apartment building. Suddenly, I heard God say, "I never forgot he kicked you." I cried the rest of that night. It was a release of the pain of the years I felt invisible and forgotten, vulnerable and afraid. God was in it for the long haul with me and He meant it. There was nothing He was going to let separate me from His love, but I had to trust Him enough to give Him access to my heart; what was healed and what was hurt. When I did He took was was healed, what was hurt, and made it whole. He can do the same for you.

Accepting Jesus isn't only about not going to Hell; it's about a relationship with God through His Son Jesus. It's about learning the truth about what love really is and having the courage to surrender your life to Him and trust to receive His love freely.

Contributing Authors

Romans 10:15

And how shall they preach unless they are sent? As it is written: "How beautiful are the feet of them that preach the Gospel of peace, and bring glad tidings of good things!"

Amie Clemonds — a dedicated boys' mama and a loving wife, she finds joy in the simple pleasures of life, especially spending time outdoors. When she's not enjoying nature or with her family, she's actively involved in her professional organization, where she's passionate about supporting others and growing together.

Pamela King – believes in authenticity, respect, integrity, strength, and excellence. As a wife, mother, and friend she has lived out those principles. She's an Iraq veteran,, sexual assault survivor, and breast cancer warrior. She commits her life to helping create a world where people are valued for their contributions, confident in their abilities, and empowered by their choices.

Nikki Randolph – is a dynamic writer, an educator, and a longtime advocate for public service. She volunteers as a mentor for several youth programs, serves in her church, and has a gift of making anyone she meets feel valued, seen, and connected to someone who cares.

Lisa Tompkins – is a certified chef, international makeup artist, and hair stylist. She has committed her life to developing the best in women and empowering them to look their best on the outside and be their best on the inside. When she's not travelling or working, she enjoys teaching beauty techniques, cooking, and spending time with her family.

Pauletta Fields – has never met a stranger. She loves to connect people to the resources they need. She is beautiful, intelligent, an artist and philanthropist who started her ministry by giving out thousands of cards of encouragement to people she would meet. Now, she's adding author to her resume.

Tameya Banks – is a visionary, community builder, entrepreneur, social networking leader, and real estate investor. She lends her time and talents to build up the next generation of leaders. As a wife and mother, she's enjoys spending time at home and travelling with her family.

Ann Bush-Curry – has lived her life serving others in the medical field, while being a wife and mother. She's a powerful teacher and minister, and a leader. She enjoys helping others and spending quality time with friends and family.

 Cynthia Roberts – is sparkling water in high heels. She's creative, joyful, travels extensively, and is the life of the party wherever she goes. She's active in her church serving in several capacities and a dedicated daughter and friend.

Stacey L. Fields – is an author, public speaker, teacher, and minister. She enjoys traveling, writing, shopping for the newest hair products, but most importantly sharing the love of Jesus with everyone she can and encouraging them to have a more intimate walk with God.

If this book has been a blessing to you, you can email:
TheBeautifulOnes2025@gmail.com

God bless you!